My First Book About

# REPTILES *ELMO*

By Kama Einhorn

Illustrated by Christopher Moroney

Random House 🏠 New York

Hello, everybodee! It is I, your furry friend Professor Grover. Today Elmo is wondering about things that wiggle and slither and creep and crawl. In other words, he is curious about REPTILES. Would you like to learn about reptiles, too? Oh, that is such a coincidence! Because that is what this book is all about, and we would love for you to read it with us.

Lizards and snakes are reptiles.
Tortoises and other turtles are reptiles.
Alligators and crocodiles are also reptiles.

saltwater crocodile

green iguana

emerald tree boa

desert tortoise

eastern box turtle

American alligator

Now remember this very important thing. Some reptiles will not hurt people, but some can be dangerous. You should never go near any reptile or animal you do not know unless a grown-up says it is okay. Okay? Okay.

Will you slither through this book with us? Say yes the way a snake would. *Yesssssss.* Very good!

# Reptiles come in all shapes, sizes, and colors.

There are almost 7,000 kinds of reptiles.

rainbow lizard

bow-sprit tortoise

That is a **lot** of kinds of reptiles!

**green water dragon**

**Sonoran Mountain kingsnake**

## TWIDDLEBUG TRIVIA

The biggest reptile is the saltwater crocodile, which can weigh more than 2,000 pounds. That's as much as a small car!

The smallest reptiles are Jaragua geckos, whose bodies are a little bigger than a half inch. These tiny lizards could sit on your fingertip!

## GROVER'S HOMEWORK

Name the colors you see on these two pages.

## But most reptiles are the same in three ways:

1. All reptiles are covered with dry scales. They are *not* slimy!

golden eyelash viper

Nile crocodile baby

2. Most reptiles come from eggs.

3. All reptiles need the sun in order to stay warm and the shade to stay cool.

painted turtles

# All reptiles are covered with dry scales.

Scales are super-thick pieces of skin that protect the reptile.

Scales can form sharp points.

**Galápagos land iguana**

Tortoises and other turtles also have hard shells that protect them. But underneath the shell, their skin is still covered with scales.

Shell

Scales

**iant tortoise**

Let us talk about scales a little bit more. Touch your fingernail. Your fingernail protects the skin on your finger. Well, scales are a lot like fingernails.

# Most reptiles come from eggs.

An adult reptile lays the eggs.

Most reptile babies hatch from eggs that are laid on dry land—that is, not in water or in swampy ground.

> Do you want to know something amazing? The shells of most reptile eggs are soft and bendy, not like the shells of chicken eggs you eat, which are hard.

**Hermann's tortoise**

> The Galápagos tortoise is one of the largest in the world. Its egg is also big!

A python will lay 30—or even more—of these eggs at one time!

Most baby reptiles live and grow in the eggs until they are ready to be born. Then they hatch.

Some baby reptiles are born live.

green turtle hatchling

A baby turtle is called a HATCHLING. This hatchling has left its shell on the sand and is ready to go into the water.

**female golden eyelash viper and snakelets**

Baby snakes are called SNAKELETS. This snake mommy kept the eggs in her body until these snakelets were ready to be born.

And baby crocodiles are called BABY CROCODILES!

# All reptiles need the sun to stay warm and the shade to cool off.

People do not *need* this, although they often enjoy being warmed by the sun and cooling off in the shade.

**yellow anaconda**

This snake is staying warm in the sun. If it gets too hot, it might go under the log for shade or into some cool water.

**GROVER'S HOMEWORK**

On a sunny day, go outside and feel how the sun warms your body. Then go in the shade and feel how you start to cool off.

Some reptiles use underground burrows to cool off. A burrow is a hole or tunnel in the ground. In colder places, reptiles might hibernate in the burrows all winter to stay warm!

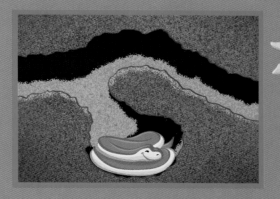

green water dragon

This lizard uses the warm sun and the cool water at the same time to keep its body temperature just right.

# Different reptiles eat different things.

**parrot snake**

Open wide! Many snakes have jawbones that can separate so that they can eat things that are bigger than their mouths. That would be like sticking a whole birthday cake in your mouth all at once!

**chameleon**

Many lizards have long, sticky tongues that can dart out and move fast to catch bugs.

## Some Things Reptiles Eat
By Elmo!

fruit
leaves
fish
frogs
worms
jellyfish
snails
eggs
ants
crickets
rodents
birds
other reptiles

**Komodo dragon**

Many snakes and lizards have forked tongues to help them eat better. They use their tongues to smell! They do this by sticking their tongues out and moving them around. And since snakes have no hands, they also use their tongues to feel.

**giant tortoise**

Would you like to know the difference between tortoises and other turtles? Okay, I will tell you. Tortoises live on land, and other turtles live in water.

This tortoise likes to eat flowers.

But they both begin with the same letter: **T!**

# Reptiles have different ways of protecting themselves.

Reptiles need to protect themselves as they hunt for food.

**panther chameleon**

Many reptiles use camouflage. They change color or use the colors around them to help them hide.

**dwarf crocodil**

Turtles can pull their bodies into their shells to hide. The shell is very hard.

**African spurred tortoise**

**frill-necked lizard**

This lizard is trying to make itself look scary so that other creatures won't bother it.

# Reptiles live almost everywhere on earth.

In oceans and seas . . .

green sea turtle

in deserts . . .

horned viper

leatherback turtle

American alligator

on beaches . . .                    in swamps . . .

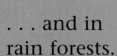
boa constrictor

. . . and in
rain forests.

# And reptiles are full of surprises!

**green python**

Snakes do not blink. In fact, they do not have eyelids, so they cannot close their eyes when they sleep!

We have learned so much about reptiles. But, Elmo, you must see this! Oh, I cannot believe my eyes. Oh, brother! Just when you think you know everything about reptiles . . . there is more!

This lizard lives on hot desert sand. So that it does not get too hot, it keeps only two of its four feet on the ground at once. It looks like it is dancing!

**shovel-snouted lizard**

**GROVER'S HOMEWORK**

Pretend that you are a two-footed shovel-snouted lizard on hot sand. Dance around to keep your feet cool.

When the outside of a snake's scales gets old, the snake can shed that skin. It comes off all in one piece, just like when you take off your sock! Underneath, there is new skin.

**yellow-bellied sand snake**

Basilisks can actually walk on water!

**basilisk**

# "EXTRA-CREDIT" FUN FOR EVERYONE!

If you want to learn more about reptiles, here are some fun things you can do with your family:

**1.** Most zoos have a reptile house, where you can get a safe, really close-up look at the reptiles. Describe which one is your favorite and why.

**2.** In the spring or summer, visit a pond or swamp and look for turtles or turtle eggs. Go to a park and look for lizards or snakes. Remember: Do *not* touch or disturb either the turtles or their eggs or any other reptiles you might find!

**3.** *S* is for SNAKE! Use Play-Doh to form an *S* shape. Now give your snake a name! Make eggs and a baby snake, too. Put your snakes in the sun and then in the shade. Make food out of Play-Doh and pretend your snakes are looking for something to eat.

**4.** Most reptile eggs are not hard like the chicken eggs we eat, but are soft and leathery. To see and feel what they are like, take a hard-boiled chicken egg and soak it in a cup of vinegar overnight. In the morning, the shell will be soft, just like a reptile egg!